FIESTA!

SYRIA

GROLIER

An Imprint of Scholastic Library Publishing
Danbury, Connecticut

Published for Grolier
an imprint of Scholastic Library Publishing
Old Sherman Turnpike, Danbury, Connecticut 06816
by Marshall Cavendish Editions
an imprint of Marshall Cavendish International
1 New Industrial Road, Singapore 536196

Copyright © 2004 Times Media Pte Ltd, Singapore
Second Grolier Printing 2006

Set ISBN: 0-7172-5788-6
Volume ISBN: 0-7172-5802-5

Library of Congress Cataloging-in-Publication Data
Syria.
p. cm.—(Fiesta!)
Summary: Discusses the festivals and holidays of Syria and how the songs, food,
and traditions associated with these celebrations reflect the culture of the people.
1. Festivals—Syria—Juvenile literature. 2. Syria—Social life and customs—Juvenile literature.
[1. Festivals—Syria. 2. Holidays—Syria. 3. Syria—Social life and customs.]
I. Grolier (Firm). II. Fiesta! (Danbury, Conn.)
GT4874.5.S95S97 2004
394.265691—dc21   2003044852

For this volume
Author: Damien Foo
Editor: Lynelle Seow
Designer: Lynn Chin
Production: Nor Sidah Haron
Crafts and Recipes produced by Stephen Russell

Printed by Everbest Printing Co. Ltd

Adult supervision advised for all crafts and recipes,
particularly those involving sharp instruments and heat.

CONTENTS

SYRIA

A large part of world history took place in what is now called Syria. Ancient tribes, powerful rulers, and the Crusaders have passed through its land. Syria is associated with both bloody battles, as well as one of the most beautiful flowers in the world – the Damascus rose.

MEDITERRANEAN SEA

LEBANON

DAMASCUS

Bosra

◄ **Damask** is a beautiful fabric that has a rich weave of flowers, fruits, animals, and other types of patterns. The name originated from the ornamental silk fabrics of Damascus, which were sometimes made from gold and metallic threads.

▶ **The ruins at Palmyra** were once the palace of a powerful woman named Queen Zenobia. Her armies took over Syria, and by AD 270 they had conquered all of Asia Minor. She was finally captured by the Roman emperor Aurelian and led through the streets of Rome in golden chains.

TURKEY

Aleppo

Palmyra

IRAQ

JORDAN

◄ **Cuneiform** is the ancient method of writing that gave rise to what we know as the alphabet. It was invented by the Phoenicians, who lived in Syria thousands of years ago. The writing consists of wedges that each stand for a sound. In Latin "cuneiform" means wedge shape.

▲ **Damascus steel** is used for handmade knives because of its beautiful wavy patterns. The Crusaders first encountered it in the eleventh century and named it Damascus steel. Unknown to them, it had come from India. The traditional methods for making Damascus steel have been lost over the centuries. Only recently have some of these methods been rediscovered.

► **The Street Called Straight** is believed to be the oldest surviving street in the world. It is located in Damascus, the capital of Syria, and is mentioned in the Bible. It was along this street that the Apostle Paul recovered his eyesight.

5

RELIGIONS

The Qur'an is the holy book of Islam. It consists of 114 chapters called surahs.

Syria is a mainly Muslim country. That is why the country's important holidays are Muslim holidays. Most Syrian Muslims belong to the Sunni sect of Islam. The rest belong to the Shi'as sect and the smaller Druze, Alawites, and Ismailis sects.

SYRIA IS LOCATED in the Middle East. Like most of its neighbors, it is a largely Muslim country. Nearly 85 percent of Syrians are Muslim. The remaining 15 percent of the population are Christians, Jews, or Yazidis. The Yazidis are a small religious group whose beliefs combine some aspects of Judaism, Christianity, Islam, and older religious beliefs.

ANCIENT RELIGIONS

Before the Muslims conquered Syria, a number of religions were followed there. The Phoenicians, Babylonians, Greeks, Romans, Jews, and Christians all practiced their own religions.

The Orthodox Christian cross is different from the Catholic cross because of the slanted line near the bottom of the cross.

ISLAM

The Prophet Muhammad was born in Mecca in A.D 570. He worked as a merchant until he was forty years old. Then he was visited by the angel Gabriel, who taught him the words and teachings of God. These words and teachings were eventually written down in a book called the Qur'an (Koran).

Prophet Muhammad began to spread these teachings in Mecca, and soon he attracted many followers. But resistance later forced him and his followers to flee to Medina. In A.D 630 he returned to Mecca but died two years later. Mecca has since become the most holy city for Muslims. Every year Muslims from around the world make their way to Mecca for a pilgrimage called a *hajj*.

CHRISTIANITY/ CATHOLICISM

The Christian and Catholic communities make up about 10 percent of the population. The major Christian sects in Syria are the Syrian Orthodox, Greek Orthodox, Armenian Orthodox, and the Roman Catholic churches. The Christian and Catholic communities are active in their religious practices. Holidays such as Christmas and the Orthodox Easter are celebrated in Syria.

GREETINGS FROM **SYRIA!**

Arabic is spoken by more than 20 million people around the world, and it is the official language spoken in Syria. Here are some simple words and phrases.

How do you say...

Hello
Marhaba

Good morning
Sabah al hayr

Thank you
Shukran

Goodbye
Ma'assalama

What is your name?
Mai ismak?

7

MUHARRAM

Muharram is the beginning of the Muslim New Year. It is set by the lunar calendar and so varies from year to year. Muharram is a time of joyous celebrations for Syrians. It is also a time to remember Islam's greatest martyr.

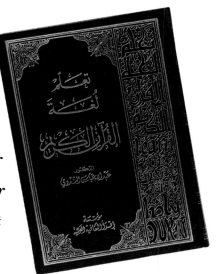

The first day of Muharram serves to commemorate the day on which the Prophet Muhammad and his followers left Medina to return to Mecca.

The mood during Muharram is festive until the tenth day of the holiday. On the tenth day Muslims fast to remember the heroic sacrifice of Imam Husayn, who was the prophet's grandson, and his faithful family and friends.

According to Islam, the Prophet Muhammad was God's final messenger. It is said that Imam Husayn inherited many of his grandfather's religious qualities. He supported the religious teachers around him by refusing to honor a ruthless tyrant,

Imam Husayn's father was named Ali. He was known as the Lion of God. That name is written here in Islamic script. When Ali died, Imam Husayn took over his position as caliph.

Desert stones were used by the enemies of Imam Husayn to stone him to death.

Muslims honor Imam Husayn because although he suffered hundreds of wounds, he did not stop praying to God. His final prayer before he died was "Accept the sacrifice of your Husayn... forgive the sinners among the faithful, O Merciful One." But his enemies showed no mercy as Imam Husayn lay dying in the desert surrounded by the bodies of his friends and family — they cruelly beheaded him.

who was named Yazid. Because of his beliefs Imam Husayn and his followers, along with their wives and children, were tortured and then brutally killed.

Imam Husayn himself was stabbed many times by his enemies before he died. His wounded body was left to rot in the Karbala Desert for several days.

Muslims find meaning in the life of Imam Husayn, who preferred to die a matyr's death rather than live a life of disgrace under his enemies. For his faithfulness to Islam he remains in the hearts and minds of Muslims. His shrine is frequently visited to this day. Muslims believe that visiting Imam Husayn's grave can help anyone give up worldly desires.

Desert winds slowly buried the slain body of Imam Husayn in the Karbala Desert.

9

EID-AL-FITR

Eid-al-Fitr marks the end of a month of fasting for Ramadan. Muslims around the world celebrate by preparing special food and visiting each other. Eid-al-Fitr is one of the most important celebrations in the country, since most Syrians are Muslim.

Syrian sweets usually contain dates, pine nuts, or pistachios. Some sweets are flavored with rose water.

The ninth month of the Islamic calendar is known as Ramadan. It is a time when all Muslims go without food or water from sunrise to sunset. Fasting is an act of great discipline; all Muslims experience hunger to remember those who are less fortunate in the world. It is also a time for devout Muslims to set their minds on spiritual improvement. Families read the Qur'an together to learn and develop themselves.

Eid-al-Fitr, which means "breaking of the fast," marks the end of Ramadan. It is a joyous occasion with plenty of festive food. For Syrians sweet treats top the list of favorites. During the day Syrians visit their relatives and friends. It is a tradition to wear new clothes so that everyone looks their best. It is also customary for children to receive money from their uncles.

On this day the streets are busy with all kinds of activities. Carnivals, horse rides, and go-cart races are organized for the children. Firecrackers are also set off as part of the festivities.

Eid-al-Fitr is officially celebrated over three days; but if these days fall in the middle of the week, shops, schools, and embassies close, sometimes for the entire week!

Muslims use calendars that also show daily prayer times and the names of the Islamic months, such as Ramadan.

HUMMUS

Hummus is a spread or dip made with chickpeas. It is simple to prepare and popular with children. It is prepared and served mostly during the Muslim holidays.

YOU WILL NEED
1 can of chickpeas
(discard half the water)
1 clove of garlic
2 tbsp sesame seed paste
Lemon juice
A pinch of salt

1 Put the first three ingredients in a blender.

2 Add lemon juice to just below the level of the peas. Add salt. Blend till smooth. If it is too thick, you can add a little more lemon juice.

Serve hummus with pita bread. Break off pieces of pita bread, and dip them like chips. Hummus is also delicious as a dip for meat.

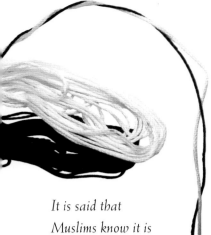

It is said that Muslims know it is sunrise when they can tell a white thread from a black one.

EID-AL-ADHA

This is a time of thanksgiving for all Muslims and a day to remember the sacrifice of Abraham and his devotion to God. It is also a day for doing charity and asking for forgiveness among Muslims.

Eid al-Adha is also known as the Feast of Sacrifice. It is an important holiday in the Muslim calendar, since it celebrates the end of the *hajj*, which is a pilgrimage to the holy city of Mecca. The *hajj* is performed by many faithful Muslims. This pilgrimage is the world's largest gathering of Muslims each year.

Eid al-Adha lasts for three days. It serves to remind all Muslims of Abraham's willingness to obey God by sacrificing his son Ishmael. Unlike the Christian and Jewish account of Abraham's sacrifice, Muslims believe that it was Ishmael, and not Isaac, whom Abraham was asked to sacrifice.

According to the Qur'an, Abraham had a dream in which he was told to sacrifice his most valued possession. He woke up and sacrificed his favorite goat, but the dream continued. He then killed his favorite sheep, but the dream still did not go away. Abraham then realized that the sacrifice

Muslims usually give a third of the sheep sacrifice to the poor, a third to relatives, and keep the remaining third for their family.

in the dream was meant to be his son. Although it was hard for both father and son, they were determined to obey God. On the day of the sacrifice Abraham blindfolded himself. His son lay before him ready to be slain. Suddenly a voice from heaven told him to look down. To his surprise, Abraham found that he had killed a ram

Eids are religious festivals, so going to the mosque to pray is important. The prayer carpets that Muslims use can be beautifully decorated.

instead of Ishmael. God told him that this had been a test of his faith.

The day of Eid-al-Adha begins with early morning prayers called *salat al Eid*. After the prayers Muslims then slaughter sheep, cows, or goats. The meat from this sacrifice is shared among friends, neighbors, and relatives. Some meat is also given to the poor. Because of this act many needy Muslims are able to enjoy meat on this day.

Families visit each other starting with the home of the eldest family member. Visits to other relatives fill up the rest of the day. Muslims also take this chance to ask each other for forgiveness for any wrongdoing done to one another.

Just as on Eid-al-Fitr, everyone celebrates by buying brand-new clothes. Children get gifts and money, which are called *eediyeh*, from older members of their families. Festive food is usually prepared and exchanged between families and friends.

THE FIVE PILLARS OF ISLAM

After the death of the Prophet Muhammad in A.D 632 his followers began to further define what it means to be a Muslim. They identified five key responsibilities for members of the faith known as the "Pillars of Islam." They are duties every Muslim must perform. The five pillars are: A declaration of faith, daily prayers, helping the poor, fasting, and a pilgrimage.

EVACUATION DAY

Syria had not tasted freedom for a long time. It had been under foreign control for most of its history. It was a great accomplishment for the nation when Syria was finally granted independence in 1946.

The United Nations was set up in 1945 to preserve peace by helping resolve conflicts between countries.

Syrians celebrates Evacuation Day on April 17, the day when the last French soldier left Syria in 1946. It was then that Syria, for the first time ever in its modern history, experienced freedom from foreign rule.

When World War I ended in 1918, Syria came under French rule. Syria remained under the French for 28 years. During this time Syrians were allowed to start taking over some government-related functions, such as tax control, social affairs, and customs. But Syria was still not independent from the French. In 1945 Syria joined the United Nations (U.N.), a move that helped it finally gain its independence.

Evacuation Day is Syria's national day. It marks the milestone in Syria's history when the last French troops were forced to leave Syria in 1946.

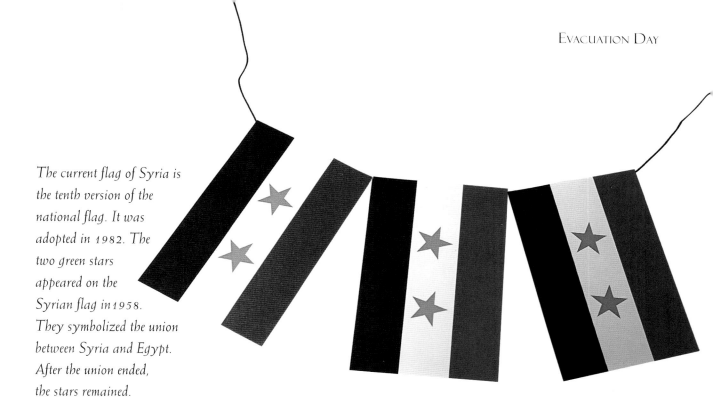

The current flag of Syria is the tenth version of the national flag. It was adopted in 1982. The two green stars appeared on the Syrian flag in 1958. They symbolized the union between Syria and Egypt. After the union ended, the stars remained.

The United Nations had stated that any U.N. member could not be placed under the control of another country. Syria claimed that the French soldiers present in their country went against this strict U.N. ruling. Other nations, including the United States and the Soviet Union, pressured France to pull its troops out of Syria, but the French refused. The British prime minister at that time, Sir Winston Churchill, threatened to send troops to Damascus to defend Syria's right to be independent. Finally, in February 1946 France was given a U.N. order to leave the country. The French obeyed, and Syria was independent at last.

On Evacuation Day Syrians hang their national flags everywhere outside their homes. In schools children make their own Syrian flags to decorate their classrooms or houses. Syrians do not celebrate their national day with big parades or marching bands. Instead, large gatherings are held in town squares to announce developments in public projects.

MAKE A SYRIAN FLAG

Many Muslim nations have similar colors on their flags; red, green, white, and black. That is because historically these colors were associated with important events. It is also said that the color green is linked to the Prophet Muhammad's cousin, Ali, who was wrapped in a green cloak when he stopped a murder attempt on the prophet. The color red on the Syrian flag symbolizes the struggle for freedom; white signifies peace; and black stands for Syria's dark colonial past.

YOU WILL NEED

*A piece of white cloth three feet across
and two feet wide
Red paint
Black paint
Green paint
A pole or stick*

1 Using a pencil, draw two straight lines across the cloth, separating it into three sections of equal width.

2 Paint the top portion red and the lower portion black. Leave the middle portion white.

3 Make a small mark about one-third along the width of the white portion. Repeat the mark at the two-thirds position. Paint a green star on each of the marks in the white portion.

4 Tie the flag horizontally onto a pole or stick.

MARTYR'S DAY

Syria's history with Turkey goes back many centuries. The Ottoman Turks took over Syria in 1516 and ruled Syria for more than four hundred years.

Martyr's Day is celebrated on May 6. It is a public holiday. This day is important since it a day to honor those Syrians who lost their lives fighting for Syria's independence. When World War I broke out in 1914, countries were separated into two groups: the Allies and the Central Powers. Turkey took the side of the Central Powers. The Allies asked the people of Syria to fight the Turks. Syrian soldiers entered the war and fought against the Central Powers. Many died. On Martyr's Day Syrians remember these soldiers. A wreath is placed in the middle of the city square to commemorate their heroism. It can be an emotional day for all Syrians.

DAMASCUS INTERNATIONAL FLOWER SHOW

The International Flower Show is held in Damascus in April or May each year. Syrians are experts in horticulture, and the Flower Show shows their talent.

The International Flower Show is an important event for both Syrians and their Arab neighbors. Many Arab countries take part in the show each year, but other countries are represented as well. It is an excellent opportunity for these countries to display their plants and new growing methods.

A large variety of flowers are on display at this colorful event. They are grouped into different sections according to the country they are from; one section may display flowers from Egypt, and another section has flowers from Iran. Herbal plants, which can be used for medicine, are also displayed along with the flowers.

The Flower Show is extremely popular with children because of the kid's drawing competition. Children win prizes for the best drawings of the Flower Show.

The favorite flower for all Syrians is the Damascus rose. So proud are the Syrians of the Damascus rose and of this special event that images from the Flower Show are often printed on Syrian stamps.

Winners of the children's drawing competition are announced during the event, and their works are displayed as part of the Flower Show.

The Bird of Paradise flower grows along the Nile River in Egypt.

MAKE A ROSE BOX

1 Mark out the center of the circular lid with the pencil.

2 Arrange the roses starting from the marked center outward. Begin with a pink rose followed by a circle of red roses and so on. Once you are happy with the design, start gluing the roses into place, and let them dry.

3 Measure the outside of the box carefully. Cut a piece of the pink ribbon to be the same length.

4 Close the lid, and carefully glue the pink ribbon onto the box just under the lid line.

5 Repeat step 4 with the red ribbon. Glue it around the lid of the box.

YOU WILL NEED
A round papier-mâché box
14 red and 14 pink medium ribbon roses
Craft glue
⅝ inch wide pink ribbon
⅛ inch wide red ribbon
Pencil and scissors

Let the box dry completely before handling. Once the box is dry, you are ready to fill it with something nice to give away to a special friend. It also makes a perfect place for jewelry and coins.

Boxes in different colors and shapes can be used. You can personalize your box by arranging the roses to form your first initial. Or you can experiment with different-colored ribbons and roses to create boxes for weddings, parties, or for Mother's Day.

COTTON FESTIVAL

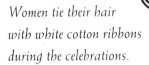

Women tie their hair with white cotton ribbons during the celebrations.

The dates of celebration can vary, but the Cotton Festival is usually held either in July or in September each year. Cotton is a very important export product of Syria. Many jobs are generated from the cotton industry.

Cotton is one of Syria's biggest exports, and the Cotton Festival is always celebrated at the end of each cotton season to welcome the year's harvest. It is held in the city of Aleppo, Syria's second largest city. Aleppo is where the main cotton plantations can be found, since it has the highest amount of rainfall of any area in the country. Cotton is used to make many things: from clothes, socks, and mittens to tablecloths and doormats.

Syrians celebrate the Cotton Festival for two reasons. The first is to celebrate good weather in the past year, and the second reason is to pray for more good weather for the following year so that there will be a very good cotton harvest.

The Syrians believe that without celebrations there would be no rain and bad crops. Everyone at the festival must try to make a lot of noise, since it is said that the noise might keep hungry locusts away from all the cotton crops.

The women of Aleppo celebrate by dressing up in their best white cotton dresses during the festival. Cars and houses along the streets are decorated with white cotton wool. Even hospitals, government offices, airports, and banks are decorated with cotton. The Cotton Festival is one of the most important events celebrated in Aleppo.

SHIEBIAT PASTRY

The Shiebiat pastry is a popular dish in Syria. It is made for all kinds of festivals and celebrations, since it is simple to prepare and delicious. Traditionally the filling is made of cream. Here we are using vanilla custard. For added variety peanut butter can also be used.

YOU WILL NEED
1 package of filo dough
1 box of vanilla custard
Scissors

1 Get a pack of filo dough from the freezer section of the supermarket. Follow the directions on the box on how to handle the dough.

2 Take a sheet of filo dough, and cut it in half. Continue to fold each half until you have one strip.

3 Make the vanilla custard filling, and cool it.

4 Put one tablespoon of the cooled filling into the filo dough.

5 Start folding one corner of the dough diagonally across to the opposite edge to form a triangle. Continue folding until you finish the strip.

6 Preheat oven to 350 degrees, and bake triangles until golden brown. Serve warm.

Filling
Get a box of instant vanilla custard from the supermarket. Follow the directions on the box about how to make the vanilla custard.

BOSRA INTERNATIONAL FESTIVAL

Syrian handblown glass is a specialty often found in the handicrafts exhibits. The usual colors are blue, green, and amber brown.

The town of Bosra is located in the south of Syria. Syrians and Arabs flock to Bosra to enjoy the festival of music and art in September every two years. Many tourists also come to enjoy the entertainment.

The famous Bosra International Festival is an event that showcases the cultural and artistic activities in Syria and the surrounding Arab nations. It is a festival for the arts, including music, culture and traditions. It is also known as the Bosra Folklore Festival.

The performers at this festival include musicians, local dancers, and street magicians. Some of these performers come from all over the world, but most are Syrians and Arabs. There are also poetry sessions and exhibitions of different local crafts.

A fascinating part of the Bosra International Festival is the place in

The rose motif appears on many Syrian handicrafts. Throughout the Middle East the rose is regarded as the most perfect of all flowers.

which the entertainers perform — an ancient Greek citadel known as the Bosra Amphitheater.

The Greeks built this large performing stage almost 1,800 years ago. The Romans later occupied Syria and continued to use the amphitheater for circus acts and gladiator matches.

This large, impressive amphitheater, which can hold up to 8,000 people at one time, was designed in such a way that the entire audience can hear the performers without the use of microphones or any other special equipment. Today the amphitheater is one of the most important landmarks in Syria.

Syrian music sounds different from Western music because it uses lots of quarter notes.

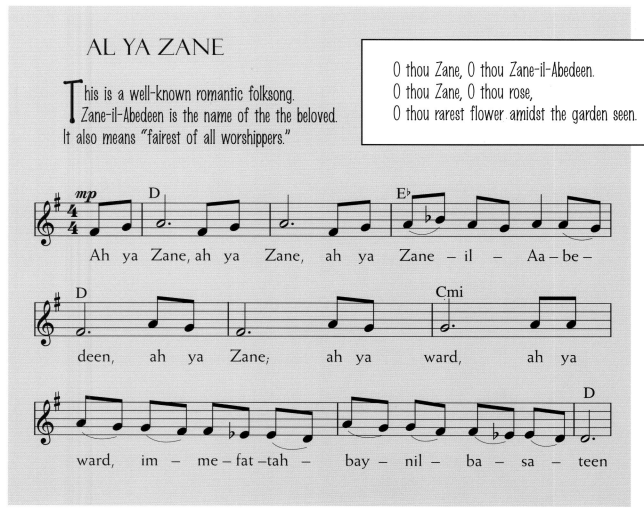

AL YA ZANE

This is a well-known romantic folksong. Zane-il-Abedeen is the name of the the beloved. It also means "fairest of all worshippers."

O thou Zane, O thou Zane-il-Abedeen.
O thou Zane, O thou rose,
O thou rarest flower amidst the garden seen.

Ah ya Zane, ah ya Zane, ah ya Zane – il – Aa – be – deen, ah ya Zane; ah ya ward, ah ya ward, im – me – fat –tah – bay – nil – ba – sa – teen

23

THE YOUNG MAN IN WOMEN'S CLOTHES

Honor is very important in Arab culture. This Syrian folktale is about a young man who pretended to be a woman in order to protect the honor of a neighbor's daughter. He falls in love with her, but he cannot reveal who he is.

THERE ONCE LIVED a sheikh who had a son named Husam. His family traveled a great distance and found a good place to set up home. But another man from the Shammari tribe also wanted to live on that land. Both men agreed to share the land. The sheikh found out that the Shammari had a daughter named Halima. Not wanting his new friend to fear for his daughter's honor, the sheikh lied and said he too had a daughter. Later that night the sheikh told his family what had happened. "You must dress as a woman from now on," said the sheikh to his son.

Husam obeyed his father and dressed himself in women's clothes. His mother braided long black silk in his hair and gave him jewelry to wear.

Days passed, and Husam and Halima soon became the best of friends. They did all their chores together, and Husam sometimes slept in Halima's tent.

One day they caught thieves trying to steal their herd of camels. They called for their fathers, who ran out to help them.

"Fight us for the camels if you can," laughed the thieves at the sight of the two old men. Fearing for everyone's safety, Husam ran to his tent, changed out of his female clothes, and armed himself with a sword. Halima was waiting outside when Husam emerged from his tent dressed in his own clothes.

"It is for you that I fight these thieves," said Husam to the surprised Halima." I am your friend, but I also love you as a man

loves a woman." When Halima heard this, she was filled with joy.

Husam fought the thieves and brought the camels back to the tent of Halima's father. But the old man's heart burned with anger.

"Why did you lie to me?" he asked the sheikh angrily. "Your son even slept in my daughter's tent!"

"Forgive me," said Husam's father. "My

son is a good, noble man. I would have killed him with my own hands if he had dared touched your daughter."

But the Shammari could not accept the sheikh's apology and left, taking Halima with him.

Months passed, but Husam could not forget Halima. Finally, he went in search of her in the land of the Shammaris. When he arrived, he discovered that Halima was to marry her cousin Ali. Husam searched

for Halima and found her in the wedding tent. The two friends wept and held each other throughout the night. Unknown to them, Ali had seen everything that had happened.

The next morning Ali went to speak with Halima. He told her that she did not need to marry him if she loved another man. When she heard this, Halima wept and thanked her cousin for his kindness.

The wedding guests arrived the next day. Ali announced to them that he would grant Halima any request she desired.

"I wish to be married to our guest Husam!" she cried.

So Ali called Husam to come forward and united him with Halima. They were married that night, and the wedding celebration lasted eight days.

CHRISTMAS

Christmas may not be as widely celebrated in Syria as in other countries, but it is still an important event for the Syrian Christian community. Like other children around the world, Syrian children receive gifts from an unseen and legendary source.

The bright star in the East led the three wise men from the Orient to Bethlehem.

Although Muslims make up a large portion of the population in Syria, Christmas Day is still a public holiday. This allows the Syrian Catholic and Christian communities to celebrate the birth of Jesus Christ along with other Christians around the world.

Syrians have a unique and interesting way of celebrating Christmas. All Catholics and Christians lock their gates on Christmas Eve. That is because there was a time in Syria when all Christian worship had to be kept secret. Christians were cruelly persecuted for their religious beliefs. The

locked gate now serves to commemorate that time of Christian suffering.

In the home the family celebrates by lighting a bonfire in the yard and gathering around it to sing hymns. Traditionally the youngest son in the family begins the evening by reading the passage from the Bible about the birth of Jesus. The father then lights the bonfire. The whole family gathers around to observe the way the fire spreads. It is said that how the fire burns

26

through the wood tells how the luck of the family will be in the coming year. Everyone then takes turns making a special Christmas wish.

On Christmas Day families wakes up early to attend Mass. Churches set huge bonfires ablaze in the churchyard. An image of Jesus Christ is then carried around the church, while everyone sings hymns.

Although there are many Christians in Syria, some of the more common Christmas practices are not followed there at all. Few families put up Christmas trees, stockings, or even decorations. Children in Syria have never heard of Santa Claus. Instead, they

The legend of the smallest camel, who brings presents for children, is told only in Syria.

believe that if they are good, the smallest camel of the three wise men will reward them with a gift on the day of Epiphany. Many children look forward to the camel's visit.

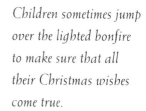

Children sometimes jump over the lighted bonfire to make sure that all their Christmas wishes come true.

THE SMALLEST CAMEL OF THE THREE WISE MEN

The star of the east brought the three wise men to Bethlehem. Following them on their long journey was a very special camel, whose faith in God is remembered by all Christian children in Syria every Christmas.

THE BIRTH OF JESUS CHRIST is one of the most celebrated festivals around the world. The story of Christmas is told over and over again on Christmas Day, but the story of the Smallest Camel of the Three Wise Men is unique only to Syria.

Long ago in the days when King Herod ruled, there lived three wise men, who were also known as "Magi." One night they noticed a bright star shining in the east. They believed that the star was a sign that a king has been born. They decided to follow the star to search for this newborn king.

The three wise men were led to a manger in Bethlehem. There they found Joseph and Mary with the infant Jesus. There were also shepherds surrounding the baby. They were called to the manger by angels announcing the birth of the Son of God.

The three wise men had traveled a long distance across the desert to reach Bethlehem. They moved across the land in a caravan with many camels. The smallest camel in the caravan was exhausted by the long journey, but it refused to give up because it wanted to see Baby Jesus. Jesus saw that the loving animal had such a strong faith that he granted the smallest camel the gift of immortality — the ability to live forever!

Syrians believe that each year the smallest camel visits good children to bring them gifts. The example of the smallest camel teachs children that even the smallest, most insignificant person is important to God.

FEAST OF SAINT GEORGE

Saint George is the patron saint of Syria and is honored by the Syrian Catholic and Christian community as a martyr. On April 23 each year devoted followers in Syria gather to celebrate the Feast of Saint George.

Saint George was born to a wealthy Christian family in Cappadocia, Turkey. As a young man, he joined the Roman army and rose quickly through the ranks. The Emperor Diocletian soon heard of his success and made him an officer.

In the year A.D 303 the emperor issued an evil imperial edict ordering the destruction of all churches and the burning of all holy Christian documents and books. Christian officers were stripped of any rank, and all Christians were to become slaves. Angered by this edict, the brave Saint George pushed his way to the middle of the city square and tore the edict to shreds. He was arrested at once, thrown into prison, and tortured horribly. But Saint George could not die. He miraculously came back to life after every attempt to kill him. The frustrated emperor finally cut off Saint George's head. Saint George was ony twenty three years old when he died.

Saint George is best remembered in Christian mythology as the saint who killed a terrible dragon. In Syria he is better known for his bravery in disobeying the emperor.

WORDS TO KNOW

Bonfire: A large fire built outdoors.

Caliph: A supreme ruler or a title taken by the heads of Islam.

Caravan: A group of travelers in a desert; usually merchants, who go together for safety.

Citadel: A fortress usually found on a hill and used to defend a city.

Commemorate: To honor the memory of someone.

Crusades: Military expeditions in the Middle East by Christians in the 11th to 13th centuries.

Cultivate: To grow a plant from seeds or bulbs.

Horticulture: The art of growing flowers, fruits, and vegetables.

Imperial edict: A command or order issued by the emperor.

Legendary: Famous because of a story handed down from older generations.

Martyr: A person who chooses to die or is put to death because of a religious belief.

Ottoman Turks: Turkish soldiers who invaded Syria in 1516.

Patron saint: A saint who protects a country or person.

Persecution: Cruel oppression of religious beliefs.

Pilgrimage: A journey made by a person to a shrine or holy place.

Pita: A small, flat bread that can be cut to form a pocket for filling.

Qur'an (Koran): A holy book containing the teachings and beliefs of Islam.

Wrongdoing: Any act or behavior that is bad.

ACKNOWLEDGMENTS

WITH THANKS TO:
Ariel Seah, Ben Yap, Iris Sin, Jamilah Mohd Hassan, Nafisah Ismail, and Niki Seow for the loan of artifacts.

PHOTOGRAPHS BY:
Haga Library Japan (cover), Yu Hui Ying (pp. 12-13 bottom left, p. 27 bottom left), and Sam Yeo (all other images).

ILLUSTRATIONS BY:
Ang Lee Ming (p. 1, pp. 4-5, p. 7, p. 25, p. 29)

SET CONTENTS